Ruins Too Bright To Visit

poems by

Donald Secreast

Finishing Line Press
Georgetown, Kentucky

Ruins Too Bright To Visit

ACKNOWLEDGMENTS

"In and Around the Bodega (Huata, Peru)" appeared in *The Purple Monkey*.
"Snow Ledges above the Ulta Valley" appeared in *Southern Poetry Review*

Editor: Christen Kincaid

Cover Art: Donald Secreast

Author Photo: Tina Greene

Cover Design: Elizabeth Maines

Printed in the USA on acid-free paper.
Order online: www.finishinglinepress.com
        also available on amazon.com

Author inquiries and mail orders:
Finishing Line Press
P. O. Box 1626
Georgetown, Kentucky 40324
U. S. A.

Table of Contents

To my daughters,
Hubi and Estee

Hills like Marble Cake

We have brought ourselves
to this unfamiliar place
with its red tile roofs
and hills marked like marble cake
under a sun which keeps our lips
dry   peeling down to the pain
of moisture.

Never establishing ourselves
in the hotel room that stays cool
in the beds made too tightly;
what we have brought with us
piles in corners   wakes us at night
shifting positions as we shift   already full
of a town after a week   our tickets
to the ruins punched   expired.

We have come to believe at last
that we are here   rely more heavily
on the regularity of meals
sitting longer in the crowded plaza
easy in our way of turning away
the campesino women who sell
bands of woven cloth or fruit or bells.

The secret is to treat them
as if they are out of place—
to make them feel
the distance afflicting us.

Following the Stone Carriers

Harvest has left the fields
in yellow stubble   and splinters;
the only green is eucalyptus, cypress,
and large heads of cabbage.

In this dry part of the country,
around every curve   someone
has routed a runnel of water
through the dust   mud bricks stacked
higher and higher beside the road.

Alpaca drowse in flocks
flanked by pigs browsing
knotted clumps of barley.

A line of stooped men
jump the creek, glancing at us;
we are tempted to call them dwarves
in sandals and serapes.

We take the path
down which they've come
later overtaken by them   one by one
each with his bundle of stones
sacked upon his shoulder   building
a wall   three miles from their quarry,
laboring as if there is no alternative
nor any need for alternatives.

Guided Tour: Pisaq to Ollantaytambo

As we wait for the van
that will take us to the Sacred Valley
of the Incas   from Pisaq to Ollantaytambo
the first shift of school children
pass in their gray sweaters and pants
the air perfectly shaped   around them
and the boy selling juice
washing his one glass over
and over in the same water.

We have already been
to the ruins important to us
those we hiked to, slept in, crawled over
all ways of meditating   knowing
you've not really been to a place
unless you've drunk hot chocolate there
in the morning   Red Zinger tea
thick with sugar   at night:
to cook in a ruin   gives back
the life that built it.

After a good lunch in Pisaq
the guide tells us
which temple is the sun's   which the moon's
how the llama was sacrificed
where the grain was stored.

By the last ruin
the wind has picked up
wavering the edges of the remaining walls
and the terraces scaled for war.

Bells for Dark Places

If you see the mummies
in the Cuzco museum
early enough in the morning
you will have all day
to adjust.

They have the same expression of hunger
every skull claims   the skin.
Even tucked in their classic fetal
position   bound in hide, ropes, basket
they seem to float   outside their restraints
beyond the limitations of decay.

You will keep returning
to the skulls   trying to make some inquiry
about what is worth preserving
caught not by eyes but by where
the eyes should be   the nose cavity
looking as if all it can smell now
is the carving of ancient blades;
the jaws, whether dropped open
or more properly wedged shut
by a fastidious mortician,
all seem sculpted from the smooth
stone of astonishment   no one
really expected to find himself here   embalmed.

What skin they have left
is the color of a cathedral at dusk,
the doorways of museums after closing hours,
blocks from the lights of cafes
where guests finger the starched napkins
wondering why they'd feel better
if bells could be hung in all dark places.

Light Walk into Old Lessons

Without the weight of food or spare clothes
we walked the four and one half miles from
Huaraz to the Wilkawain Temple
in about an hour and a half,
feeling for the first time since our arrival
that we were in a foreign country.

On the road much like a riverbed
sheep passed us without a bleat
one dog barked   more distracted
by the lamb bouncing around him
in mimicry of his agitation with us.
Donkeys eating cactus   benignly
ignored us;   a man with a small hoe
chopping watercress in a small stream
smiled at us   children called us gringos
in voices like chocolate wrapped in silver.

Eucalyptus held the air   draped
from the Cordillera Blanca
like a rime-haired girl
lifting a bridal veil;
the odor from white mountains
made us talk about elementary school
our first books about places
illustrated in ink   often in silhouette.

Then the temple itself   not a ruin
watched over by a boy with atrophied calves
below in the valley   a woman and a boy
thresh grain with limber pipes of polyvinylchloride.
Another woman chops in a circle of stumps
all action slow and thoughtful
like the working of some large domestic brain.

Halfway back to town, we wonder
what has happened to us
our feet are sore and all we want to do
is eat and sleep   as if we have become
those old women who stood up all day
teaching us an alphabet
we just overtook   today.

Sleeping Between Glaciers

Pass between glaciers
and part of them will follow you.

All you can do after supper
is look at the stars
more tangible
than the ground you sleep on
as they move, multiply, then wash away.

Slower than clouds
the moon barely solid rises
gliding like relief
through what your eyes
have gathered of the sky.

In the morning where you slept
stiff with ice   rustles
like a hint of infirmity
until dawn finally touches camp.

You see the moon has dissolved
leaving its skin stretched
across the valley   back up
where the glaciers are stored in themselves.

Laguna Taullicocha

La Punta Union de Santa Cruz is a pass
almost 16,000 feet high
and you have to feed yourself
a lot of chocolate to climb it.

By two o'clock in the afternoon
and halfway up the mountainside
you realize the pass isn't anywhere near
where you thought it'd be   not veering
toward the left   but straight across
bald rock   loosely balanced cairns
showing you where to walk   your brain
unsteady at this altitude   your feet
slip and jar the ringing in your ears.

This is more than work   more than vacation
you almost know what it is when you reach
the final hundred feet
of ascent built of black stones
like the entrance to a castle
built by the engineers of the Inquisition.

When you pass through the gap
thousands of feet high   five feet wide
you almost expect to see what you do—
valley as far as vision can follow
mountains retracting their glaciers
and a lake whose color
if made into a serum
could cure
the entire population of disappointment.

The Fissure of Santa Cruz

If you pack up your wet tent
at eight o'clock and walk for an hour,
you'll come to a meadow filled with stones
perfectly shaped for spreading out
all of your damp possessions because by now
you've caught up with the sun.

This will be the last chance
you have to rest and appreciate
the scenery   if you want to get out
of the valley before dark,

Because now,   your skin feels thinner
than when you started and you think
part of you is slipping into
the Laguna Grande   the whole valley
tilts you toward it and walking is all
that holds your parts together.

If you don't stop for lunch
if you don't stop to lotion yourself
against the small flies that bite
and bring your blood out in red dots
if you don't stop to remember the canyon walls
or to do something for your feet
you can reach Cashapampa by four
in the evening   where children will tell
you the bus leaves in the morning.

Two beers later   drunk in a yard
Adorned with a lugubrious truck
a man will offer to drive you down
for an outrageous price
which you gladly pay
because it is getting late
and all day the fissure of the Santa Cruz
has been threatening to swallow you.

Sunday Afternoon in Huaraz

A good watermelon
always fulfills the promise
it makes when you split
it open after you've already eaten
more than you needed to

Like a Sunday afternoon
by a river in Peru
where women in derbies wash
their week of clothes
pounding them with wooden paddles

The hems of their skirts
getting damp   their eyes dark
as the seeds in the center
of your watermelon   you divide
your time evenly between extracting
seeds from pulp and watching
the women load their baskets
piece by piece   with clean shirts
dresses, pants   the sun flashing
on the water   on your spoon   on your neck

Until you finally scoop to the rind
and its taste of immaturity
reminds you of an afternoon
when you walked out in the grass
wearing your first suit
and a pair of white shoes
that hurt your feet perfectly with newness.

Pucallpa

It is hard to tell
if this town is rising
from the mud   or sinking
in it.   The jungle is certain
of its acreage
despite the men
who have ordered drainage pipes
and tin roofs   laying
their plans in and out of the rainy season
a weaving as bright though not
as permanent as the cloth ornaments
on the bows and spears   sold
by Indian women to people
eating chicken joints in the Chinese
restaurants   drinks come to you
wet from ice boxes   you thought
had been replaced   except in your childhood.

Recollection   teased by the mildew
you smell whenever you lie face
down in your hotel bed
the fan touching your back like mosquitoes
but still cooler than you expected
in a room whose paint cannot hold
against the humidity when evening comes
like a damp towel left too long
against a feverish forehead

Streets receive the rain
scheming
to make something green of it.

Iquitos, after a Night of Rain and a Day of Clouds:
To a Girl Married to a Millionaire

Maybe because I cannot speak
to any of the women here do they
make me think of you whom I have not
spoken to in nearly three years—
although I saw you a year ago   your new Fiat
pulled off the side of the road
where you walked to the fruit stand
no doubt to buy some special fruit
to surprise your husband with   you
always could do much with what
little you picked up along the way.

This town with no roads
to the outside world is mercifully
free of white Mercedes and golf   and that helps
me keep your husband bearably vague
as he is in person   blurred
by his constant association with his parents'
money   I like to be in places
where I'm sure he would be unhappy
as I was today on a crowded bus
riding to Lake Quistacocha   sitting
beside an old woman in a dirty dress . . .

Even after two bowls of ice cream
I can still feel her soiled warmth
against my side   these people seem to know
no reluctance to touch.

Then my faults come to me
my lack of generosity   how I resent
the way people will pack into a place
how when I looked for my sister's gift
I bought the cheapest silver bracelet I could find.

At the Hotel Sangay, Banos, Ecuador

The hotel dining room
is white tablecloths and green
glasses turned upside down   waiting
for your hunger and thirst.
The napkin fits to your lap
like the shade from a tropical leaf.

The light comes from the woman
at the table next to you   her voice
is low   linen washed by the waterfall
hung in the sun at noon   dry
by three, before the rain
drops over the mountain of eucalpytus.

Her eyes make your silverware heavy
as your rising suspicion of the waiters
coming from the kitchen without a backward glance,
your food balanced on their fingertips
as if service isn't enough without a performance
or dinner sufficient without courtships.

Ecuador, from Quito to Guayaquil

1

Friday night in Quito
a modest earthquake and a bomb
set off in a textile factory, but you've already
made arrangements to leave in a Mercedes bus
with black curtains and blue fringe around
the ceiling lights; the road swerves through
tall grass, bamboo, palms, bananas   passing
a small truck, a girl in back   holding down
her skirt   combing her hair; a child
beside her eats an orange   makes a blossom
from the chewed, turned-out pulp.

2

Vendors clamber aboard whenever the bus slows
boys with plastic bags of cola, men with enamel
trays stacked   slices of scarcely peeled pineapple.

3

Coconuts and potholes
until all gives way
to banana groves or grass
jungle churns to horizon
as clouds whisk themselves   platinum.

4

Over the curving bridge, the main street
of Babahoyo, you are reduced to your armpits
and skeletal system
water   five or six inches
deep everywhere   houses on stilts Brahma bulls
browse in swamps   up to their knees in hibiscus.

5

Then the ocean bluffs   dusk
taxis   rain   without effect
through the air of grit and gauze

all of it outside where you bathe
before the storm
boats knock against the docks
dark syncopated blossoms opening all night.

Where Atahaulpa Once Sat

On the small hill above Cajamarca
is the place to eat breakfast
where Atahaulpa once sat to think
about himself and his empire   never
guessing   this would be the town
where he would be strangled by Pizarro
after paying the conquistador two rooms
of silver for his freedom up there
where the larger gray and pink hills
wear the altitude like dancer's tights:

Fruit you've been craving,   first an orange
to take away the dryness of the climb
then a papaya with lime juice   the acid
turning the cheap metal of your knife black—
when you peel the apple, the corrosion
smudges the yellow   the brown pulp
but it is still good always the taste
of autumn and golden leaves even in a town
without seasons   the landscape
can betray itself with a fortune of brightness.

Always the Potatoes

A cab ride from Cajamarca to the Cumbemayo ruins
costs thirty dollars and lasts
for twelve miles   rocks bumping almost
through the floor of the climbing car.

You stay in the ruins long enough
to take pictures, sit in the mouth
of the rock carved like a head
and get turned around   wandering
an hour before following the road
to Chetellian and from there to San Pablo

Once over the pass   the road
divides into dozens of paths   all
looking like shortcuts   though
not necessarily to where you're going.

Fog slides down the valley   you pass
six women sitting in a circle in a field
of wheat guarded by two dogs   the women
look identical through the fog   their dark
skirts and shawls   their straw hats
with the high flat crowns   they ignore
you at first then one points through
the fog in a direction she thinks
you should take   but you only get lost
enough to know you are lost   and start
back   meeting a man on horseback

who tells you to follow him. "Perdido,"
he says over his shoulder   as he cuts
off the trail across a grassy stretch
his three dogs sniffing you then loping
back into the mist and bushes   one always
staying by your guide who is as wide
as the animal he rides and who picks
his way slowly down the rock and mud path

that has appeared like another dog out
of the fog turning to rain but the man
is in a charcoal poncho a straw hat
and on his rubber boots are spurs
which he never uses because the slope
you're descending makes that kind of encouragement
redundant and this man knows the world

contains enough redundancy because at the farm
on the edge of town, he points to a freshly turned
field and says, "Las papas. Siempre las papas."

In and Around the Bodega (Huata, Peru)

You walk to Huata on a day when you don't
mind risking sunburn because it seems unavoidable
with the sun everywhere   on the brown
Santa River   on the dust of the road
on the green of the plants until all of them
have grown spines or thorns or barbs
and when you do come to shade it is
almost audible   someone slapping shut
a book to get your attention   when you step
into it   you expect your ears to pop.
This sunlight weights your boots like mud;
only the yellow butterflies are happy
in it   drunk, fluttering on it   you
feel closer to the gray butterflies cluttering
in aerial columns over damp places where
a trickle of water crosses the road.

In the one bodega Huata boasts
filled with amateur taxidermy trophies—
an owl   a hawk   two bats   a crow
two shrews in combat   a ferret eating a sparrow
a deer head shaped like a cushion
songbirds suspended from the ceiling like models—

A man all whiskers stoop and grease
followed by a girl barely larger
than some of the creatures
suspended from the ceiling
comes in carrying a dead animal in a sack
which he trades for a pound of cocoa leaves
one cigarette   a shot of Anisado   but before
he drinks his clear alcohol, he makes sure
his daughter has one piece of candy   by then
you're ready to go   step into the heat
that has been waiting   in the distance
cows shimmer like ruins too bright to visit.

Snow Ledges Above the Ulta Valley

The blue of the snow ledges is not the blue
of the sky   not the sky that opens
and closes in clouds as you walk
up the Ulta Valley   hoping the light sprinkle
tapping on your nylon jacket will pass
before you stop to camp in the meadow
below Ulta and Hualcan's white
serene severities   separated by a glacier
that spreads toward the valley in scallops
down to the boulders bunched like sheep.

The snow ledges are the blue
of the half moon's mascara
what a blond woman would wear
when she really doesn't want
to wear it   and wouldn't except
all her occasions now are formal.

This is the blue of a sound
that keeps you awake in a place
you'll visit only once   the wind
palpitating your tent   layering above
then below the passage of the river
a form in a gown whose fabric
is not meant to follow every twist
of flesh only those turns most easily
held onto   as light in its failing
trajectory hangs from those ledges still blue
when you have put on your long underwear
and sweater and zip yourself into
a bag that in the dark could pass
for silk   for the blue of the snow
for the taste of water at four o'clock
in the morning for the memory you have
of a woman you last saw five years ago.

The Nazca Lines

Over your bowl of cream
of tomato soup   you see two
women lead Maria Reiche
who wears a gray sweater
and a red scarf   stooped
from her study—30 years—
of the Nazca Lines.

You've ridden the bus seven hours
from Lima to hear this woman
talk   sitting by the pool
at the National Tourist Hotel
under a full moon with the air
cold as the source of all angels
forcing everyone to sit with arms
buried against stomachs   crouched
with tribal intensity to hear
the old woman talk about measurements
and answer questions without looking
at who asks them   her audience
is merely a reminder of certain truths:

"They found a graveyard with thousands—
millions of graves . . . I'm not exaggerating . . .
all you see are bones . . . good pottery . . .
the finest glass in the world . . . one
carbon 14 test was performed on a stick
and dates about 525 a.d., but the figures
are much older . . . when you go flying
tomorrow you will see much destruction
car tracks are everywhere . . .
I have a book I sell which helps me
pay for caretakers and three motorcycles—
there are no cars there now . . . I charge
ten dollars for tourists but if you don't
have the money, I will lend you the book."

Soon she retires across the tile bricks
to her room next to the desert
containing those ancient doodles
composed of moon lines   sun lines
and solstice lines which always add
up to something significant   beyond
the shivering group drifting
toward separate rooms   already dreading
the bus ride back tomorrow afternoon.

No Tombs   Just Trees

Your first visit to a convent provides relief
from the city and the pity you felt
for the pious women who shut themselves
or were shut away from the temptations
which are such a large part of your identity.

Of course   Santa Catalina isn't typical
designed for the rich and aristocratic daughters
of Arequipa   usually, the guide tells you,
the second daughters who had no prospects
of marriage because the first was given
the dowry   but still the convent required
a donation   the size of which determined the size
of the young nun's room   some had houses.

The last nuns' names are carved over their doors:
Dolores Llamosa Domingo Somocursio Maria Josefa Cadena
the Mother Superior who had her own toilet brought
from Italy   her own washing machine from Germany.

The walls closest to the outside world
are painted orange to signify impurity—
the middle walls are blue for heaven
and the inner walls where the oldest
nuns lived are red   sacred blood,
but between the blue walls
three crosses are planted
surrounded by five orange trees
scarlet geraniums growing everywhere
indigo morning glories   cultivated   cascading
over walls   you are led from the Locutorio
where nuns talked through a wooden trellis
to their family   to Noviciado where
the initiates spent 18 or 19 months preparing
themselves by studying 55 paintings of church doctrine.

All of the beds were placed under arches
in case of earthquakes   from speakers
Toccata and Fugue reverberates as you are led
by   De Profundis   the wake room where
two dead nuns at a time could lie
before being carried to the Cemetario
where each nun planted a tree in the spot
where she wanted her grave   the guide points
to the closed door of the cemetery
directly across from the place
where clothes were washed and the maids bathed
and says "No tombs   just trees."

Cross or Follow

The valley is full of water and plants
that want you to help in their proliferation;
brown burrs stick from your shoulders down
to the waistband of your pants   green flat
seeds chevron your sleeves
while your boots and legs get soaked
and when you do top a ridge touched
by the sun   you suffocate   in the old air
trapped in the lattice work of palms sealed
by webs braided from ferns—
fronds uncurl toward the sky like the black
knots of a heart wanting to be influential.

The whole mountain against which you walk
down to the Huarinilla River   but
this far above it all that reaches you
is its rasp of damp friction   close
to the leaves that you push through
a sound you have been between
for three days now except when
you've dropped into those ravines
where smaller waters have been practicing
their songs   where briefly the stream
you cross   silences the stream you follow.

The Market and Volcano, Zumbagua, Ecuador

Goats are skinned as soon as they are sold,
their blue flesh more graceful with the matted wool
taken out of the way; next to the butcher
the man with the biggest audience uses a loudspeaker
to auction off plastic buckets from the back
of his truck,   his voice echoes from the Andean hills
some of them   out of hearing   too high in stone
their need for commerce eroded long ago—
others, patched green and gold with cultivation
bend the noise, the light, the fallen waters
down to the river   down to the deep crevices
floods have cut twenty   fifty   a hundred
feet into the plain until the only continuous path
leads to Quilota   the volcano   the crater
half a mile across   instantly wipes out
the eight miles you've walked and climbed
its lake seven hundred feet below   the color of extinction
with only clouds for relief and the grass
that has found its way down the slopes
fits like gums over the water.

You sit on the lip of spectacle and zip your jacket
eat a chocolate bar to recuperate.
Such sights make you incomplete   divide your
comprehension
because this volcano escapes you   won't be encompassed
by your admiration   or compromised by your fatigue.
You don't have it in you   to circle its rim.

Back to the bus through the rain
children drive their sheep to shelter
you wonder how they can leap in the drizzle.
A boy follows you behind a black hog—
he can barely see over its haunches.

This is the memory that settles in on the drafty ride
back down a road turned white with snow
fallen from a thunderstorm: those two hurrying
on small feet toward their separate ideas of home.

Donald Secreast teaches composition, fiction writing, and literature at Radford University. In the summers of 1982 and 1983, he traveled through Peru, Ecuador, and Bolivia with Charles Frazier who was working on his travel guide *Adventuring in the Andes*. Although Secreast didn't contribute a great deal to the travel guide, he did outline a collection of short stories while on a long bus ride from Caraz to Lima, and the collection was published as *The Rat Becomes Light* by Harper & Row in 1990.

Presently, Secreast is working on a book entitled *Catching the Narrative Wave: Using Microsoft Excel to Teach Close Reading*. He has demonstrated this technique at CEA conferences in Virginia and Puerto Rico. The publication with which he is most satisfied is an essay about how to introduce students to analytical topic sentences: "Physics for English Majors: How to Construct a Death Ray for Generalities," which appeared in the Fall 2009/Winter 2010 issue of *The Virginia English Bulletin*.